CRAZY HORSE

Chief Cunningham...

Chet Cunningham

Lerner Publications Company
Minneapolis

This book is gratefully dedicated to my wife, Rose Marie, who is the rock, the solid foundation, who never complains, and who keeps the household on a happy and even keel.

Front cover: There are no known photographs of Crazy Horse because he never allowed himself to be photographed. The image on the front cover shows the 1876 Sioux and Cheyenne encampment near the Rosebud Creek, just before the famous Battle of the Little Bighorn, in which Crazy Horse led his people to victory against the U.S. Army (led by Lieutenant Colonel George Custer).

Lerner Publications Company
A division of Lerner Publishing Group
241 First Avenue North
Minneapolis, MN 55401 U.S.A.

Website address: www.lernerbooks.com

Library of Congress Cataloging-in-Publication Data

Cunningham, Chet.
    Chief Crazy Horse / by Chet Cunningham.
      p. cm. – (A&E biography)
    Includes bibliographical references and index.
    Summary: A biography of the Oglala leader who spent his life fighting to keep the white man from taking over Indian lands.
    ISBN 0-8225-4978-6 (alk. paper)
    1. Crazy Horse, ca. 1841–1877—Juvenile literature. 2. Oglala Indians—Biography—Juvenile literature. 3. Oglala Indians—History—Juvenile literature. [1. Crazy Horse, ca. 1841–1877. 2. Oglala Indians—Biography. 3. Indians of North America—Great Plains—Biography.]
    I. Title. II. Series.
E99.03 C72213 2000
978.004'9752'0092—dc21
[B]   99-37845

Manufactured in the United States of America
1 2 3 4 5 6 – JR – 05 04 03 02 01 00

CONTENTS

Outraged Indians attacked pioneers' wagon trains moving along the Bozeman and Oregon Trails as they crossed the Indians' prime buffalo hunting range in the mid-1800s.

Chapter **ONE**

THE BATTLE OF THE HUNDRED SLAIN

IF YOU HEAD NORTHWEST FROM SOUTHEASTERN Wyoming into Montana, you'll find what is known as the Bozeman Trail. In 1866 the United States Army opened this trail, which led through prime Indian hunting lands.

In the 1800s, settlers streamed from the eastern United States to the "unoccupied" lands of the northern Great Plains. The trail dug into lands that the U.S. government had promised to the Indians in treaties. The treaties had guaranteed this land, which the Indians had long inhabited, to the Indians.

The Indians who lived in the area were furious and gathered together to fight this wrong. Crazy Horse's tribe, the Oglala Sioux, was part of the group. The

7

Sioux attacked and harassed the settlers moving west, forcing them to seek refuge in the forts that the army had built to protect travelers. Soon, no traveler dared to ride his horse or pull his wagon along the Bozeman Trail. So the Indians turned to attacking the forts.

One fort, called Fort Phil Kearny, was built on a grassy plateau near Clear Creek, about thirty miles from the Wyoming–Montana border. The fort was surrounded by a fence of logs driven into the ground and tied together, with the tops sharpened into points. The Indians could not scale the tall pole fence. So instead of trying to capture the fort, they watched it, attacked and chased any troops that came out of the main gate, and waited.

Occasionally, the soldiers sent wagons to the nearest forest, five miles away, to bring back wood for cooking, for heating the fort houses and barracks, and to continue construction on the fort itself. Sometimes, Crazy Horse and his raiders attacked the soldiers at the woodlot, wounding and killing them and their horses. Soldiers' repeating rifles, which could be fired up to fifteen times without reloading, soon drove the Indians away.

The Indian war leaders decided on a strategy. Using themselves as decoys, they would lure a large group of soldiers out. Twice, excited young warriors attacked too quickly, before the soldiers were in the trap, and the soldiers had galloped out of danger. Then twenty-five-year-old Crazy Horse was chosen to lead the decoy. Crazy Horse handpicked his team—he was

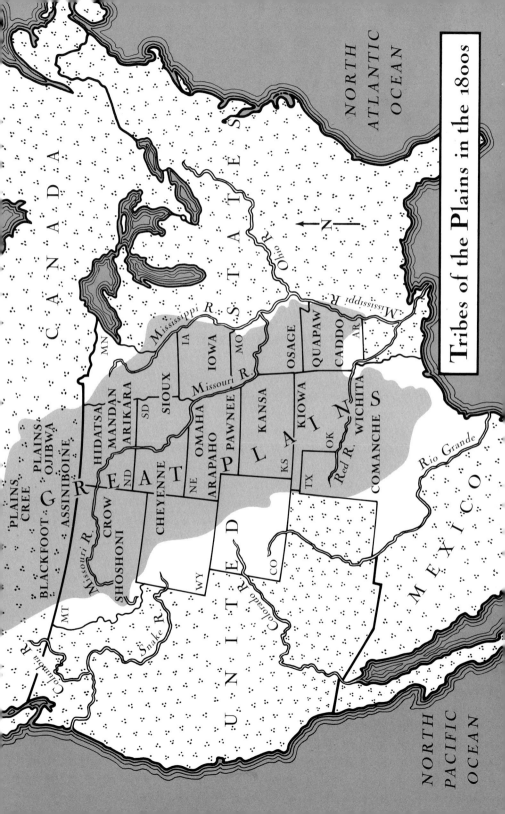

Tribes of the Plains in the 1800s

NORTH
ATLANTIC
OCEAN

N

NORTH
PACIFIC
OCEAN

CANADA

UNITED STATES

MEXICO

GREAT PLAINS

PLAINS CREE
PLAINS OJIBWA
BLACKFOOT
ASSINIBOINE
CROW
SHOSHONI
HIDATSA
MANDAN
ARIKARA
SIOUX
IOWA
IA
MN
SD
ND
MT
WY
NE
CHEYENNE
ARAPAHO
OMAHA
PAWNEE
KANSA
KS
CO
OSAGE
QUAPAW
CADDO
AR
MO
KIOWA
WICHITA
COMANCHE
OK
TX
Red R.

Mississippi R.
Missouri R.
Missouri R.
Ohio R.
Mississippi R.
Rio Grande
Colorado R.
Snake R.
Columbia R.

Sioux warrior Pawnee Killer fought alongside Crazy Horse in the Battle of the Hundred Slain.

determined not to make the mistake the other young warriors had made.

On the morning of December 21, 1866, a group of soldiers left the fort in horse-drawn wagons to collect firewood along a creek. When the soldiers got to the creek, Indian warriors charged down from the hills toward the woodcutters. The soldiers gave the distress signal by making a circle with their wagons and signaling with mirrors for help. When the soldiers inside the fort saw the signal, a troop of eighty cavalrymen organized quickly. In command was Captain William J. Fetterman. He had bragged that he could defeat the entire Sioux Nation with just eighty men. Fetterman had just gotten out of the fort when the Sioux warriors broke off their charge and disappeared into the forest.

At the same time, another group of Sioux warriors, this one led by Crazy Horse, surged out from the grasses near the fort where they had hidden during the night. Two cannon shells fired from the fort exploded nearby. Crazy Horse and his men began to fade back into the safety of the grass and brush.

When Fetterman saw the first group of attackers in retreat, he stopped his troops. It would be difficult to find the Indians in the forest. But nearby was a group of Sioux hidden in the grass, practically out in the open. At last, he could catch some of the hated Indians.

The ten warriors in Crazy Horse's group acted as though they were retreating. Crazy Horse took off the blanket he was wearing and waved it at Fetterman, catching his attention.

Some of Fetterman's soldiers rode horses and some were on foot, so they advanced slowly. The warriors saw this and intentionally slowed their "escape," while staying out of rifle range. As Fetterman's troops moved toward the Indians, Crazy Horse leaped off his horse and examined one of its hooves as if the mount were injured. Then he shook his head and began leading his horse away from the soldiers. The rest of Crazy Horse's men closed in around him to protect their leader. The soldiers drew closer. Bullets began to whistle over the heads of the warriors. Some rounds kicked up dirt near their horses' hooves. Crazy Horse watched the soldiers closing in and, at the final second, leaped on his horse and rode fast out of range toward Lodge Pole Ridge. The warriors rode only fast enough to pull the soldiers with them.

Fetterman had been ordered not to chase any Indian groups beyond Lodge Pole Ridge—but this was an opportunity not to be missed. His eighty rifle-armed soldiers were closing in on ten Indians armed only with bows and arrows. Fetterman committed to the pursuit, urging his mounted men forward and rushing his foot soldiers into a run over the top of the ridge and down into Peno Valley. Fort Phil Kearny was out of sight.

Two thousand Sioux, Cheyenne, and other warriors were hiding on both sides of Peno Creek waiting for the signal to attack. When all of the soldiers were well over the ridge and inside the valley, Crazy Horse's group gave the signal—they broke into two parts, angled away from each other, then came back and rode across each other's trail.

The warriors rose from their hiding spots. They streamed arrows and bullets down at the surprised troops, then charged down the hills from all four sides, smashing the soldiers with war clubs, hatchets, and lances. The soldiers had little time to prepare, and few fired their weapons. It took less than an hour for the entire army force of eighty men to be killed.

The victorious Indians stripped the soldiers of their clothing, their weapons, knives, and boots (the leather could be used for making moccasins and quivers to hold arrows). They took scalps—by Indian custom, the man who killed an enemy could take his scalp as a trophy to tie to his war lance. One of the soldiers, Private Adolf Metzer, was not stripped or scalped. He was laid out on a blanket, fully dressed, a buffalo robe spread over him. The Indians had seen him showing remarkable courage and fighting skill, and this act was the Indian way of showing the ultimate respect of one warrior for another.

The Indians lost thirteen men, some from arrows fired from other warriors across the valley. One of the Indian casualties was Crazy Horse's childhood friend Lone Bear. Angry and grief-stricken, Crazy Horse vowed that he would fight the whites for as long as he lived.

The Indians picked up their dead and wounded, and hurried away to mourn their losses and celebrate a great victory. To the Indians, this was remembered as the Battle of the Hundred Slain. To the army, it was known as the Fetterman Massacre and the worst defeat the army had yet suffered by the Indians.

A Sioux mother and her children rest in front of their tepee.

Chapter **TWO**

BOY ON THE PLAINS

CRAZY **H**ORSE **WAS BORN IN THE FALL OF** **1841** **TO** the Hunkpatila band of the Oglala tribe of the Sioux Nation. At the time of his birth, his band was camped near a stream called Rapid Creek in the Black Hills. Sioux babies were often given names based on their physical appearance. Later in life, they would receive a formal name after an act of bravery or a mystical experience. So, upon his birth, Crazy Horse was affectionately called Curly Hair.

Curly Hair looked different from the other Sioux children. He had a narrow face, light skin, and soft, curly light-brown hair. People said he got his light skin from his mother, a Brule who died when Curly Hair was very young. The Brules were a tribe within

ORIGINS

A t one time, the homelands of the Lakota Sioux were around the headwaters of the Mississippi River, in what has since become Minnesota. By the eighteenth century, armed with white men's muskets, the more aggressive Ojibwa Indians drove most of the Sioux to the Missouri River and then farther west. The Sioux, in turn, attacked the weaker Plains Indians, pushing them out of the territory. The Sioux then settled across the Plains, controlling the land between the Missouri River Valley and the eastern part of what has since been known as Wyoming, and between the North Platte River and the Yellowstone River. We know this region as the states of Montana, Wyoming, Nebraska, and North and South Dakota.

the Sioux Nation. Crazy Horse, the boy's father, was the holy man of the Hunkpatila band, or subgroup, of the Oglala tribe. He was respected for his good advice and wisdom. As was customary among the Sioux, men had two wives. When Curly Hair's mother died, his father's second wife became Curly Hair's mother.

Curly, as he was also called, was a member of the Lakota Sioux, the largest branch of the powerful Sioux Nation, a nation known for its skilled hunters and warriors. The Lakota were divided into seven tribes—the Oglala, Brule, Hunkpapa, Minneconjou, Two Kettle, Sans Arc, and Blackfoot—all independent but

Left: *A papoose, as the Sioux called a baby or small child, sleeps on a cradle board.* Right: *A Sioux woman stretches a buffalo hide on a frame and cures it by drying it in the sun.*

connected by marriage, customs, and a government structure for protection. The Sioux, like some other Indian nations, lived in the northern Great Plains, a flat, grassy expanse west of the Mississippi River.

Like other Sioux tribes, Curly's Oglala tribe was made up of several small bands—family groups and friends numbering from fifteen to fifty. The bands camped near each other and traveled together when they moved from winter to summer camps following the buffalo. Each band had a chief, but the chief did not have absolute authority. Before the whites came and spread their ideas, the concept of having a single leader was foreign to the Sioux. The Oglala tribe had several leaders who were responsible for various aspects of tribal leadership. Besides the seven elected "Big Bellies," elders who were recognized as the tribe's leaders, there were "Shirt-Wearers" who executed Oglala policies fairly, and "akicitas," or tribal police, who were usually comprised of master hunters and warriors.

Nearly every summer, the tribes of the Sioux Nation gathered in one large council to form policy for the whole group, and approved or disapproved actions taken by some of the tribes during the past year.

A sprawling Oglala Sioux camp

Traditionally, the Sioux were hunters and gatherers who lived by what they called "the chase"—following buffalo herds. This provided them with food, clothing, and shelter. They lived a seminomadic life—in the summer they sometimes moved as often as every two weeks if they needed to supply fresh grazing land for their herds of horses.

Since the late 1700s, horses had become indispensable to the Oglala way of life. Before horses were brought to the Americas by the whites two centuries earlier, Plains Indians had used large dogs as pack animals, limiting the distance they could walk in a day. The horse opened up the prairie. With good horses and good weather, the Indians could easily move camp one hundred miles away—and their warriors could venture as far as two or three hundred miles to make a raid.

Only since the early 1800s had the Sioux understood the concept of owning territory. They had learned it from the whites. The structure of Sioux communities had also changed during that time, since whites had been trying to get the Indians to have a single representative for each tribe. The whites may have felt that an individual would be easier to control.

Curly and his older sister and younger brother grew up as most Indian children did—with a great deal of freedom and affection. Sioux Indians did not yell at or spank their children. They had assigned chores, but mostly they roamed around the camp, going in and out of any tepee that captured their interest. Other members of their band were like parents to any of the children. Sioux children did not have formal schooling but learned by observing adults.

Curly was a serious and quiet boy and kept largely to himself. When he was old enough to ride, his father, Crazy Horse, gave him a pony. Crazy Horse taught Curly to ride—and he was a natural. Soon he was better than most of the other boys. Like the rest of the Indian boys, he learned the techniques of fighting while riding a horse. He learned to cling to one side of the horse, hanging on to a strap around the horse's belly—that way he could shoot from under the horse's neck, where an enemy could not see him. He learned how to pick up a downed friend, how to switch horses, and how to shoot a bow and arrow from a horse. The boys had mock battles where they would charge a grove of trees, then break off and race away.

Often, Sioux boys paired off in close friendships that became lifelong hunting and battling partnerships. Curly was thrilled when High Back Bone, or Hump, as he was called, chose Curly as his *Kola,* or partner. Hump, who was a few years older than Curly, had already developed excellent warrior skills. He had chosen Curly over other boys from more prestigious backgrounds, including sons of chiefs, who had also shown potential battle skills. This was a great compliment to Curly, who benefited from the training and help that the older boy gave to him. They became inseparable.

Curly received a different sort of education from his father. In addition to teaching him how to ride, Crazy Horse taught Curly how to distinguish different bird-calls, how to read animal behavior and movements to find water, and how to read tracks and animal droppings.

The Oglala boys idolized the young Oglala warriors who went on raids and came home with scalps and horses they had captured. As the warriors rode around the celebration circle after a battle, they would recount their victories and brag about their own brave feats, displaying the scalps they had taken. The women would shout the warriors' names, and excited little children rushed after them, screeching in delight. Curly watched the parade and talk at the victory fires, hoping that someday he would be a warrior—protecting the camp and going on lightning-fast raids to enemy camps. The boys also hoped to fight the U.S. Army soldiers who were slowly invading Indian hunting grounds.

When Curly's grandfather was young, white traders and settlers from the East began to steadily stream through Sioux lands. Traders had erected several posts in the Great Plains—along the Missouri and North Platte Rivers. Indian tribes began gathering outside the buildings to trade buffalo robes for items that at first were luxuries to them but quickly became items they depended on—rifles, gunpowder, blankets, tobacco, steel knives and needles, and iron kettles.

Twice a year, Curly's band joined other Oglalas for a

Indian traders camped outside Fort Laramie, Wyoming.

long trip to the white man's trading post at Fort Laramie, which had been established in 1846 on the Laramie River. Curly watched how some of the Indians traded their ponies for the white man's whiskey. He watched the white men cheat hunters from other bands out of their buffalo hides after a few drinks of the *mini wakan,* the water that makes men foolish.

At the same time, white settlers migrating from the eastern states were heading west along the Oregon Trail—the long trail that led from Missouri across the Great Plains to the West Coast. The trail had been created so settlers could travel to the rich farming country in the Pacific Coast states. At first the Indians were curious about the *wasicus,* these pale-skinned people in their big clumsy wagons. Then more and more settlers came on the trail. In the summer, the line of wagons extended for miles. Soon the Oglalas and the other tribes became worried.

The emigrants brought with them devastating diseases such as cholera, smallpox, and measles. These diseases were new to the Indians and killed thousands of them. The livestock that traveled with the wagons overgrazed, often destroying the range surrounding the trails. Whites chopped down all of the trees and brush near the trail to use for firewood.

As revenge for this kind of destruction in many areas of the Plains, the Indians began a widespread, steady harassment. They made small-scale raids for white settlers' property such as horses, cattle, guns, and food. The Indians also stole horses and weapons from army soldiers who had been sent by the government to protect the traders and settlers.

The government couldn't control such a large area and was beginning to tire of the incessant Indian raids. So in 1851, the government sent runners to all the Indian tribes in the northern Plains area, promising them gifts of food and guns if they would come to a great council. The runners told the Indians that they would talk about peace—but what the government actually wanted was to establish Plains areas where members of each tribe would live and hunt, removed from where whites were traveling, trading, and prospering. That

OGLALAS' FOOD

n good times, when there was plenty of food, the Oglalas ate three times a day. Other than their staple buffalo meat, they also enjoyed deer, elk, antelope, bighorn sheep, pheasant, grouse, quail, and rabbit. One of their delicacies was dog meat—it was reserved for ceremonies and important events.

Indians also ate wild turnips, which grew widely on the Plains. As large as big apples, the turnips could be eaten raw or in stews and soups. If the turnips were abundant, the Oglalas would gather, slice, sun dry, and then store them in parfleches (storage boxes) for use in the winter months when the ground was frozen. The Indians would also occasionally harvest plums, currants, buffalo peas, onions, and fox grapes.

year, ten-year-old Curly, with his father, sister, and brother, journeyed to the Great Fort Laramie Treaty Council at Horse Creek, a site just east of the fort.

More than ten thousand Indians—the Sioux, Cheyenne, Arapaho, Mandan, Hidatsa, Assiniboine, and Arikara Indians, among others—traveled to Fort Laramie that summer. Longtime enemies such as the Sioux and their foes, the Crows and the Shoshonis, camped side by side. Most of these Indian tribes had never met or even seen each other except in deadly combat.

In early September, government commissioners and Indian leaders sat on buffalo robes inside a huge council tepee. Curly didn't understand the talk in English but later found out that the government wanted to establish a lasting peace on the Plains. The commissioners unfolded a grand plan to accomplish this peace. Each of the tribes would be assigned a section of the Plains where its people would live and hunt. Each tribe would stay on its land and must promise not to make war on other tribes, the army, or any of the white settlers or miners.

For several days, the leaders of different tribes met in their tribal councils. Curly crowded in close to the council so he could hear what the chiefs were saying. They were surprised and angered that the government wanted to split up their hunting lands and force them to stay in a relatively small area. Boundaries marked across the open prairie made no sense to the Indians. As hunters, they must follow the game wherever it went.

But they also knew that peace with the whites was necessary. After days of talking over the treaty, many of the chiefs signed it—though they knew that the terms would be impossible to live by. Not raid rival tribes? Then how could a warrior hone his war skills? How could he command respect if he made no raids and had no wars to fight?

It was an impossible treaty. The ten thousand Indians broke camp and many of them headed back to their home rivers and valleys, not to the areas that the treaty said they should occupy.

Horses were among the Indians' most valuable possessions.

Chapter **THREE**

THE YOUNG WARRIOR

AS THE OGLALA BOYS GREW, MANY CHOSE TO become warriors. To hone the skills they needed, the boys practiced shooting buffalo and catching wild horses. When Curly was eleven years old, he killed his first buffalo by shooting it with four arrows while riding next to it at breakneck speed. When Curly was twelve, he and some boyhood friends went to chase a herd of wild horses on the nearby Plains. Curly caught one of the horses with his rawhide rope, and, before the afternoon was over, he had broken, or made submissive, his first wild horse—it walked on a lead as Curly led it into the Oglala camp. With great pride, Crazy Horse and Hump gave Curly a new name, His Horse Looking. But this new name did not stick.

THE BUFFALO: LIFEBLOOD OF THE OGLALAS

The buffalo (bison) was the lifeblood of the Plains Indians. The shaggy animals provided the Indians with much of what they needed to survive. The Oglalas wasted almost none of the buffalo—it was used not only for food, but also for clothing and tools.

After a buffalo hunt, the Indians would cook great slabs of the meat by skewering it on a stick and hanging it over an open fire from a tripod made from poles that were tied at the top. The meat was also cooked in a cooking pouch made from the tough lining of a buffalo's stomach or from a piece of the hide. The Indians tied the corners of the pouch to the tripod and then put in the meat, water, and vegetables. Into this, they dropped hot rocks that would soon cause the water to boil. After the pouch was used for three or four days, it would become soft and soggy from the hot rocks. Then the Indians simply ate the pouch.

Sometimes, instead of cooking the meat, the Indians would cut it into narrow strips and hang it on drying racks in the sun to turn it into buffalo jerky that would keep for months. They often pounded the jerky into a powder and combined it with berries and fat to make pemmican. They stored this nourishing food in parfleches and ate it during the long winter months.

The Indians made clothing from buffalo hides. They staked down and stretched the hides in the sun and carefully scraped away all traces of meat and fat. Then they tanned the hides with buffalo brains and other materials to make buffalo robes, which would keep the Indians warm in the winter. They also used some of the tough tanned skins, or leather, to make moccasins, and quivers to hold arrows.

The Oglalas used buffalo hooves to make glue, which they used to attach feathers to arrows. The buffalo's sinews (tendons) became strong threads, cords, and bowstrings.

The young Oglalas watched warriors preparing for raids on neighboring tribes, nearby white settlements, or the wagons on the Holy Road (as the Indians called the Oregon Trail). The warriors painted their faces and bodies, tied their hair, stripped down to only breechcloths, decorated their ponies, braided their ponies' tails, and sang battle songs. They believed these rituals would protect them in battle. Many of the young boys yearned to go along on a raid. Some hid close to the warriors and listened to them make plans for a fight. Sometimes boys slipped away from their parents' tepees and rode out late at night to try to catch the war party. If they did, the warriors had a decision to make. Usually they sent the boys back to camp.

Occasionally, one of the thirteen- or fourteen-year-old boys was allowed to come along. He didn't participate in any of the fighting—he was there to gather firewood, make camp, and tend to the horses. But the boy was thrilled just to be allowed to go along. Once a boy had made such as trip, it was easier for him to be accepted on another. Curly probably went on several of these raids when he was a young boy.

The Sioux had a celebratory tradition called the Sun Dance, thanking *Wakan Tanka*, the Great Spirit, for everything the Great Spirit had given the people. Various Sioux tribes gathered for the festivities with relatives from other tribes. These were great occasions for Curly and other boys to test their speed with foot and

The annual Oglala Sioux Sun Dance ceremony lasted several days. To show their courage and bravery, young men often inflicted severe physical pain upon themselves. Then they danced around a sacred pole until they could communicate with the Wakan Tanka (the Great Spirit).

pony races. They had endless contests for jumping, running, arrow shooting, wrestling, and testing their strength and agility against one another. The Sun Dance also provided the warriors an opportunity to test their ability to endure excruciating physical pain without crying out. This test involved ritual piercings,

dancing, and fasting for many days. Quiet and reserved, Curly watched but did not take part in these
displays of courage, even though it was customary for
those who may soon become warriors to participate.

In 1854, when Curly was almost thirteen, the Oglalas
camped near Fort Laramie. In August, Curly visited
the Brules' camp, where he stayed with relatives from
his mother's side. More out of playful mischief than of
maliciousness, a young Brule warrior shot an old, de-
crepit cow belonging to a man from a Mormon wagon
train. Furious, the Mormon owner stormed over to the
soldiers at Fort Laramie to complain. Hugh B. Fleming,
an inexperienced officer, sent for several Brule leaders, including the Brule chief, Conquering Bear. The
whites had chosen him to be the main representative
of the tribe because he had long been friendly with
them. There was a heated discussion. The Brules refused to turn the warrior over to the army and instead
offered the Mormon his pick of the chief's finest
horses. But the Mormon, too, refused.

Soon Second Lieutenant John Grattan was dis-
patched to the Brule camp. He took with him twenty-nine
soldiers, two howitzer cannons, and an interpreter.
Grattan demanded that the Indian who had shot the
Mormon's cow be handed over. The warrior still would
not come out of his tepee and surrender to the army,
and Conquering Bear still refused to turn him over. Mean-
while, hundreds of Indians, including Curly, gathered
on a bluff overlooking the camp to watch the soldiers.

After much shouting and harassment by the whites, some of the soldiers fired into the Brule camp. Conquering Bear fell to the ground mortally wounded.

Shocked and horrified, furious Brule warriors wielding arrows, spears, and war clubs charged out of the camp and, within a few minutes, slew all the soldiers. Curly saw it all. He saw the blood gush from Chief Conquering Bear's mouth after he had been shot. He saw the furious Brule warriors attack and kill the enemy soldiers. Later that day, he rode with his uncle Spotted Tail as the Brules pulled up their tepee stakes, packed everything, and traveled to the north. On a horse-drawn travois, a vehicle made of two trailing poles with a platform on top, lay the wounded Brule chief, hovering near death.

This scene deeply affected the young Oglala. He knew it was time to have his vision—the spiritual, mystical message that male Sioux teenagers were expected to have. To bring on the vision, the young men were to perform various rituals with the guidance of a holy man. This vision quest was the most serious step a young boy could take—its outcome would guide his future. It would tell him if he was to become a warrior, medicine man, holy man, hunter, or anything else.

Curly decided he was ready to begin his vision quest at that moment. So, without performing the customary preparations, the thirteen-year-old Oglala traveled by pony to the sacred spot, a butte (hill) above the Platte River. Curly had none of the offerings that were

Along with other Brules, Curly's uncle Spotted Tail fought the white settlers but later supported peace between the whites and the Sioux.

usually brought—tobacco, sweetgrass, or white sage. He just knew it could take four days without food or water, while praying and asking for the vision.

Then he began doing what he had heard was done on a vision quest. He set stones in a straight line north and south, and another line east and west so they crossed in the center. He stood there a moment, then walked to the end of the four lines of stones and prayed at each one. He repeated each prayer four times. Then, since a bird of prey often becomes a messenger of the spirits, he watched the sky for birds. After an hour of praying, he waited for something to happen. Nothing did. He tried repeatedly, watching, searching for any Plains animal to appear to him. When darkness came, he sat on sharp stones so he would not fall asleep. The night was long and lonely. By the third day of performing these rituals, he was weak and he nearly fainted from hunger. He began to think that he was stupid and arrogant—a fool for not doing the vision quest the right way.

By midafternoon on the third day, he had decided to stop, feeling he had failed. With his stomach churning and his head spinning from lack of food and sleep, he stood and began to stagger down the hill to his pony—but fell into a faint. As he rolled against a tree, he felt a lifting of his spirits, a great wonder crept through him, and his eyes opened.

Curly's vision became exceptionally sharp; everything was more vivid and brilliant than in nature. He saw a rider with an unpainted face and long brown hair galloping on horseback toward him from across a lake, floating over the water. The rider warned Curly never to wear a warbonnet (a feathered headdress) and never to paint his horse or tie up its tail in the traditional Sioux way—even though these were sacred rituals warriors undertook before a battle. He should sprinkle his mount with dust, then rub some of the same dust over his own hair and body. He should wear a hawk's feather in his hair and a small brown stone tied behind one ear. After a successful battle, he must never take any goods or prizes from the fight for himself—no horses or even a scalp.

As the rider reached Curly, hail spots appeared on the rider's body along with a small streak of lightning on one cheek. He wore only a breechcloth for his battle dress. Out of the shadows came enemy fire of bullets and arrows. They stopped inches from the rider or missed him entirely. He was unscathed.

Curly awoke to find his father and Hump standing

over him. He shook his head and sat up, slowly coming back to reality. Crazy Horse's worried expression slowly faded. He and Hump had been searching for Curly for two days. Crazy Horse scolded his son for being selfish and foolish, and then took the boy back to camp.

Curly decided not to tell his father about his vision—not yet. One thing was definite though: his destiny was to become a warrior and maybe even a war leader. He knew that it was his duty to his tribe and to all the Sioux—he would defend his people and fight their battles. But he knew he would have to wait; he was still too young to fight.

The next year, when the young Oglala was fourteen, he again visited the Brule tribe. He convinced his uncle Spotted Tail to allow him to go along on a horse-stealing raid into enemy Pawnee and Omaha land. As was customary, he was there only to help the older fighters.

But during the raid, he found himself watching an Omaha warrior slipping through some brush toward the Brule warriors. Curly pulled his bow and aimed a steel-tipped arrow. He waited for an open shot and then fired one arrow. A moment later the Omaha warrior cried out, straightened, and fell motionless.

Knife in hand, Curly hurried forward, eager to take his first scalp. To the Sioux, a scalp was a badge of great honor. It represented not only victory but also courage and reverence for the human spirit. By taking the scalp, Curly believed he would share the power of the defeated warrior who had put his life in jeopardy for the good of the tribe.

But when he lifted the long hair of the dead Omaha warrior, Curly was surprised. He had killed not a warrior but a young woman. Quickly, Curly put his knife away. Killing women in battle was not shameful, but still he hesitated. He remembered his vision quest—he was to take no scalps in battle. He turned away and let one of the Brule warriors claim the scalp. They teased him about it all the way home, but he remained withdrawn and quiet.

Late that summer, Curly was still with his uncle's band in the Brules' camp. One day, he ventured out on the Plains to chase a herd of wild horses. He tried all morning, but he didn't catch one to break and so returned to the camp. Even before he arrived, he sensed something was wrong. There was too much smoke over the camp area. Then he smelled the overwhelming stench of gunpowder.

Curly rode hard until he came to a slight rise where he could look down on the circle of Brule tepees. The camp was destroyed. Fires still burned on tepees and stacks of parfleches. Dozens of people lay dead in the camp.

Earlier that day, General William S. Harney—a veteran of several Indian wars whom the Sioux nicknamed "the Butcher"—and his soldiers had surrounded the Brules' camp and launched a surprise attack. Harney was operating under the assumption that any Indian found off government-designated land was hostile and fair game for a surprise attack. Eighty-six Brules—mostly men—were killed, and seventy women and children were captured. Only a few Brules escaped.

Finding his relatives' camp destroyed and so many people dead choked Curly with bitterness and rage. The sight haunted him.

Curly searched for anyone who was alive. At last he heard moans and found a young woman hiding in the brush. She was a Cheyenne, an ally tribe of the Sioux, visiting the village with her husband, who had been killed. Curly made a travois, tied it to his horse, and laid the wounded woman on it. They traveled north, following the trail left by the few Brule survivors. The next day they found the survivors, most of whom were wounded. Among them was Spotted Tail, wounded by two pistol shots.

The brutality of the massacre would live with Curly and shape his life purpose, hardening his anger and unwillingness to give in to the whites. He vowed to protect his people and their freedom for the rest of his days.

Many Indians, including the Sioux, used sweat lodges (saunas) to purify themselves. They often added crushed, dried medicinal herbs to the water to create healing vapors.

Chapter **FOUR**

TESTING THE VISION

DURING THE SUMMER OF **1857** THE SIOUX HELD A grand council at Bear Butte, just north of the Black Hills, to discuss a policy to combat the whites. All of the tribes were there except the Brules—they had suffered too much. Curly went there with his Oglala band, the Hunkpatilas. The council decided that if the Sioux were united, they would be strongest. Together, they could defeat any group of men the army threw at them.

After the council, fifteen-year-old Curly and his father built a traditional sweat lodge to purify themselves in its warm, scented vapors. Here, Curly told his father about his vision quest.

As Curly recounted his vision, Crazy Horse's wonder

and excitement increased with every detail. When Curly had finished his story, father told son that he had truly experienced a great vision that would enable him to become a great leader of the Oglalas and all the Sioux Nation.

Crazy Horse asked his son to repeat his description of the vision over and over. At each point Crazy Horse stopped Curly to discuss every detail. Crazy Horse was most excited when Curly told him about the hail spots on the rider's body and the fact that all of the enemy bullets or arrows stopped short of hitting him.

His father explained to Curly that he was the man riding the horse, and that he must go to war only in the manner that his vision showed. Most important, he must not profit in any way from a battle or a raid—he must take no horses or scalps. His father explained that the vision meant that these directions were his magical shield—enemy arrows and bullets could not hurt Curly as long as he took no personal benefit from victory.

Curly was sixteen by that time, a man by Oglala standards and ready to take his place in warrior society. He was slight of build—a few inches shorter than most of the warriors. His hair was lighter than other Oglalas', though not as light as it had been when he was a child.

That fall and winter, the Oglalas were at peace with the other tribes. The U.S. Army did not come in

The Oglala Sioux believed that placing their dead high up in a tree would bring them closer to the heavens.

search of them. Curly had no chance to test out his vision in a battle.

The next summer, buffalo around the Oregon Trail had become scarce, and the Oglalas moved northwest. During the move, Curly decided that it was a good time for a horse-stealing raid. This type of raid was considered to be a way that the warriors could sharpen their fighting skills. Also, at the end of a raid, the captured horses were divided among the warriors. The number of horses a warrior owned demonstrated his wealth.

Curly asked his friends Hump and Lone Bear, his brother Little Hawk, and a few other young warriors

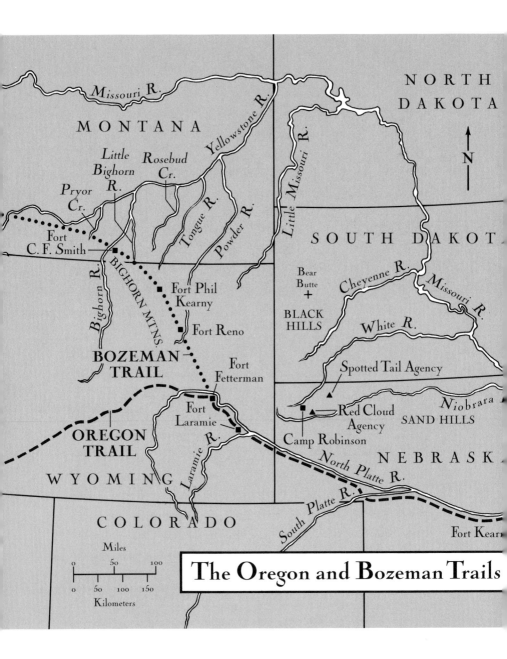

The Oregon and Bozeman Trails

to join him. The group rode ahead of the long line of Oglalas to the northwest—to the lands of their Shoshoni and Arapaho enemies. They found an Arapaho village with a large number of fine horses.

The warriors dressed in battle costume, each with his own war paint and sacred objects to keep him safe. Curly followed the directions in his vision: he wore only a breechcloth and tied a small brown stone behind his ear. A single hawk's feather stuck in his hair and a small red lightning bolt decorated his cheek. He used berry juice to put a dozen light blue hail spots on his body, as he had seen in the vision. He sifted sand over his mount and more sand into his own hair. He was ready for battle.

The raiders were spotted, and the Arapahos quickly set up to defend their village. Time after time, the Oglalas circled the defenders, but they were well hidden behind rocks and could not be dislodged. The battle seemed to be going in the Arapahos' favor.

Finally, in an act of courage and strength, Curly charged forward by himself straight at the enemy stronghold, turning the tide of the battle. Surprising the defenders, he broke through. He touched three enemy warriors with his hand or bow before charging out the other side. This was called counting coup—touching an enemy with one's hand, bow, or battle ax without killing him. It was considered a very honorable and brave act.

The Arapahos fired bullets and arrows at Curly as he

raced by them. He was surprised that the Arapahos had so many firearms. They must have traded for them or captured them from an army patrol they had defeated. Curly rode through the hail of bullets and arrows without a scratch, just as his vision had suggested. He was thrilled at the idea that no bullet or arrow could hit him.

Curly rode back to his men, then whirled and charged forward again. This time more of the Oglalas went with him, and Curly killed two of the defenders. He leaped off his pony and, in his frenzy, took a scalp—only to be struck in the leg by an Arapaho arrow. The sound of the guns frightened Curly's pony and it ran away.

He looked back at the Arapahos, then ran stumbling and hobbling down the hill, where he dove behind some rocks to safety. Hump ran over to his friend, cut out the arrow, and bandaged his leg. Curly realized that in his battle frenzy, he had forgotten the message of his vision. When he took something for himself, the power of his shield had left him. He vowed to himself that he would never take another scalp.

The Sioux warriors attacked again, this time defeating the Arapahos. The Sioux returned home with a small herd of good horses. Other than Curly, none of the warriors had been wounded.

That night, the warriors who had participated in the raid entered the light of the campfire circle and dramatically bragged about their daring deeds. But the quiet and private Curly did not. Twice they pushed him into the circle, but both times he declined. Instead, the others boasted of his courage and described how he had won the day.

Curly's father questioned the other warriors. The next day he circled the village singing a song that told of Curly's bravery and his great magical shield that had stopped any bullets or arrows from hitting him. The song ended with his father awarding Curly his new name. From that day on Curly would be called Crazy Horse, as his father and his grandfather before him had been called, and his father would be called Worm. Some said that by giving his son his name, Worm might also impart some of his magic, his holy-man knowledge, and his wisdom to his son.

The Crow Indians were bitter enemies of the Sioux. Some Crow
warriors are shown above.

Chapter **FIVE**

WAR AND PEACE

THE PEACE BETWEEN THE WHITES AND THE SIOUX in the late 1850s continued. There were plenty of game and buffalo north of the Platte River, and most of the Oglala bands continued to follow the buffalo as they moved deeper into the country to the headwaters of the Powder River, country that was still unsettled by the whites.

Occasionally, the Oglalas had small fights with their old enemies, the Crows and Shoshonis, as they battled for the bountiful Powder River hunting grounds. By 1859, eighteen-year-old Crazy Horse had become a favorite leader of these fights. Each leader of a raid would choose his team of accompanying warriors. Crazy Horse often included Hump, Lone Bear, and

Little Hawk. He had no trouble finding others who wanted to go along to share in his battle successes.

As a sign of respect for Crazy Horse's good judgment, bravery, and war skills, the akicitas—the Crow Owners Society—invited him to join them. Their job was mainly to guard the people and to strictly enforce tribal laws. Members had a private lodge where they would meet to talk, smoke, and joke together.

During these good times, Crazy Horse was in his early twenties. There were plenty of days for him to train his war pony, to make new bows and arrows, and to build his reputation as a warrior leader. At 5 feet 8 inches tall and weighing around 140 pounds, he was still smaller than other warriors. He lived with his parents, brother, and sister. Always independent and reserved, he let his actions on the battlefield speak for him.

Around this time, Crazy Horse became smitten with a young woman in the Bad Face band, a band that had split off from the Hunkpatilas some years earlier. Black Buffalo Woman was the niece of Red Cloud, the Bad Face chief and a rising leader among the Oglalas. She had soft dark eyes, a pretty face, and a wonderful smile accented by midnight black hair that spread around her shoulders when she let it loose from tight twin braids. The two young people had known each other since they were small children.

Crazy Horse regularly rode to the Bad Face camp to meet the girl at her parents' tepee. Often there was a line of young men waiting to court her with their courting blankets. A couple would stand close together and pull the courting blanket around their heads so they could talk privately. Black Buffalo Woman could slip out of the blanket at any time she wanted to and wait for the next suitor. One of her serious suitors was No Water, a young warrior in the Bad Face band.

In the summer of 1862, Red Cloud set up a large war party to move against the Crow Indians. Warriors from many of the Oglala bands volunteered to go along, including Crazy Horse, Hump, Lone Bear, Little

Red Cloud was considered one of the greatest Oglala Sioux warriors and chiefs.

Hawk, and No Water. They were a day into their journey toward the Crows when No Water complained of a terrible toothache, and Red Cloud sent him home.

Two weeks later, the war party came home and Crazy Horse received the shocking news that while the party was away, No Water had married Black Buffalo Woman. Rumor around the camps was that Red Cloud had arranged for the deception so No Water, who, unlike Crazy Horse, was from a prominent and influential family, could marry his niece.

Grief-stricken, Crazy Horse did not go to the warriors' victory celebration that night. For three days he retreated into his family's tepee, where nobody would disturb him.

By the summer of 1864, the United States Civil War was raging as the North and South battled into the fourth year of the conflict over states' rights and whether people could own slaves. That didn't stop hundreds of thousands of settlers from turning off the Oregon Trail and slicing through the heart of Cheyenne hunting grounds. This land had been dedicated to that tribe in the Laramie Treaty of 1851. The miners and settlers killed off game in a wide swath and destroyed the grazing land for the Cheyenne hunters.

In response to such treaty violations, Indians from several tribes, including the Oglalas, made renewed lightning raids into the area—hitting wagon trains, stage coaches, stations, and some ranches before vanishing into the vastness of the prairie.

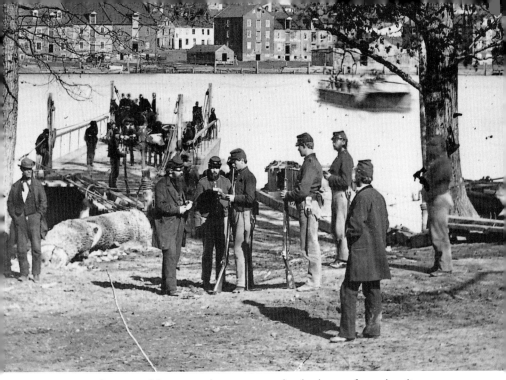

Civil War soldiers get their passes checked at a ferry landing.

The U.S. Army provided what protection they could to the settlers, but their ranks had thinned when they sent most of their troops back East to fight in the Civil War. The army was replaced with hastily gathered and mostly untrained militia. Many of them were described as undisciplined Indian haters ready for a fight. The militia would regularly storm into the countryside and attack any Indian village they saw, killing everyone in sight.

In September of 1864, Cheyenne Chief Black Kettle and several other leaders arranged a truce with Governor John Evans of the Colorado Territory. They set up a peaceful Indian camp at a small stream the Indians called Sand Creek. The army pledged to protect the camp. Black Kettle put up a large American flag and a large white flag of truce in front of his tepee to announce to the world that his was a peaceful Indian settlement.

But a few weeks later, the governor issued a proclamation that amounted to free license for whites to kill any Indian they could. On November 29, Colonel John M. Chivington, the military commander of Denver and a fervent Indian hater, decided to act on this proclamation, vowing to kill as many Cheyennes as he could—men, women, and children alike. Leading six hundred Colorado volunteers, in what amounted to an untrained mob of men who shared his view of Indians, Chivington attacked the peaceful camp at Sand Creek. By the time the fight was over, more than 150 Cheyennes—most of them women and children—were killed and their bodies mutilated. Then the whites burned tepees, took the Cheyennes' herd of ponies, and divided them among themselves.

The survivors of the Sand Creek Massacre escaped on foot and ran until they found other Cheyenne camps. Cheyenne runners hurried to all their Indian allies across the Plains—among them the Oglalas and the Brules—spreading news of the peaceful settlement's massacre and demanding revenge.

Though many whites applauded Chivington's "heroic" deed, many others, especially whites in the East and in humanitarian groups, condemned the attack. But this massacre helped the Plains Indians in a way—they began to unite against the whites.

In the winter of 1864–65 the vengeful Indians began a campaign to strike back at the whites who had so savagely massacred the peaceful Black Kettle camp. The ambitious Crazy Horse, by this time a well-respected war leader, rode south to the South Platte River accompanied by dozens of other Oglala warriors. Many Brule and Arapaho warriors joined them. Throughout January of 1865, the Indian raiders burned ranches and stagecoach stations, drove off cattle and horses, destroyed telegraph poles and lines,

An artist's rendition of the Sand Creek Massacre shows frightened Cheyenne women and children hiding while warriors and soldiers are fighting.

and killed many more white people than Chivington had killed Indians at Sand Creek. When they were satisfied, the Oglalas and other Plains tribes moved deeper north to the wilderness of the Powder River country where there were no army forts, no gold seekers, or other whites.

The government, embarrassed because it couldn't stop the raids, claimed the Indians were out of control and hurried army reinforcements to Fort Laramie. From there, soldiers could be sent into the Powder River country to confront and conquer the Indians.

But first the army had to relocate the "Laramie

Government agents distributing food rations to the Sioux Indians in Dakota Territory

Loafers," the two thousand Sioux Indians who had begun to live permanently around the fort. The army called them loafers because they lived on government food and clothing handouts, and did no work. The Sioux tribes were not critical of the loafers. One of the principles of the Sioux way of life was that each person could relocate to another band or tribe—or live anywhere he or she wanted to live.

The loafers were friendly by army standards, but just to be safe, the army decided to move them. They would put them under military escort and take them three hundred miles east down the Platte River to a fort in Nebraska Territory.

When the Laramie Loafers learned what was to happen to them, they sent runners to their relatives in the Powder River country asking for help. Crazy Horse led one of the war parties that responded. The war parties attacked the small military escort. Many of the warriors had rifles they had captured or received in trade for buffalo hides. The soldiers were outnumbered and outgunned. The army detachment was soon thwarted by the Sioux as the two thousand loafers escaped. Most hurried north to rejoin their old tribes.

In the summer of 1865, twenty-three-year-old Crazy Horse watched as the tribe's seven Big Bellies announced their four chosen Shirt-Wearers, warriors who would help enforce the elders' tribal laws. Being named a Shirt-Wearer was one of the highest honors a young warrior could receive. Typically this honor was granted to sons of chiefs. Officiating at the announcement was the greatest of the Big Bellies, Old-Man-Afraid-of-His-Horses.

The chiefs of the warrior society rode around the Oglala camp, and each time around they called out the name of one of the chosen Shirt-Wearers. The first three were sons of the Big Bellies. To everyone's (including his own) surprise, the last one called was Crazy Horse, whose father was well respected but not a chief.

In the ceremony, Crazy Horse and the others were taken to the center of the council lodge, which had the sides rolled up so everyone could see. The four new Shirt-Wearers sat on buffalo robes facing the Big Bellies. Every man, woman, and baby in the tribe was there for the induction ritual. First they had a fine feast of roasted buffalo and dog meat. Then each of the new Shirt-Wearers was given a new shirt made from sheepskin and dyed with traditional blue-and-yellow or red-and-green designs.

The sleeves and backs of the shirts were fringed with locks of human hair, each one representing a brave deed the warrior had done. These included saving the life of a fellow warrior, woman, or child, counting coup, taking a scalp, capturing a horse, taking a prisoner, or being wounded. Crazy Horse's shirt was said to have had more than 240 locks of hair.

One of the elders of the tribe told the new Shirt-Wearers their responsibilities. Their primary job was to preserve order. They would also lead the warriors in camp and on raids. They would protect the rights of every Oglala, especially the weak, poor, widowed, and orphaned. The elder announced that these warriors had been chosen because they were strong, brave, just, and generous.

Crazy Horse's demeanor did not change when he became an official leader among his people. Though he was a Shirt-Wearer, he seldom went to the councils, and when he did go, he almost never spoke. He still kept to himself, avoided speaking with adults, but often told children tales about the glories of the Oglalas that he himself had heard as a child.

Rich gold deposits in Montana and Dakota Territories attracted many fortune-seeking whites. The Indians staged many attacks to expel the intruders.

Chapter **SIX**

THE BOZEMAN
TRAIL FIGHTS

IN THAT SAME SUMMER OF **1865,** THE **U.S.**
government made a move against the Sioux. The army
wanted to teach the Sioux Nation and their allies a
lesson—that they couldn't attack the army and U.S.
civilians without suffering serious counterattacks.
They also wanted to open and keep open the Bozeman Trail to Montana Territory. Gold had been found
in Montana's mountains, and the gold rush was on.

The government well knew that the trail cut through
the longtime Sioux Powder River hunting grounds.
The trail extended from Fort Laramie across the Pow-
der River, along the eastern edges of the Bighorn
Mountains, and then west through the Bighorn and
Yellowstone Rivers, ending in Virginia City in the

Montana Territory. The officials knew the Indians would not stand by idly. The government sent General Patrick E. Connor along with two thousand troops to the Powder River area where the Sioux were living. Connor was known as a tough man who followed his superiors' orders stringently. He was to acknowledge no flags of truce or talks of peace with any Indian. He was to attack every village he found and to kill every male Indian over twelve years of age.

But the Indians were determined to defend their home territory, and Connor was disorganized and made many mistakes. The Indians spotted, tracked, and trailed the general and his men. The Indians knew of the soldiers' whereabouts at all times. Occasionally, a warrior band of Indians would attack a patrol, a wood-gathering group, or the fringes of the large camp. Soon the Indians began to raid the soldiers' camp and would run off with many of the army's badly needed horses. Then, without a trace, the Indians would fade away into the Plains, leaving Connor and his men without a trail to follow and thus no chance of catching the attackers. This routine went on for days and then weeks.

Finally, Connor abandoned his mission and retreated to Fort Laramie. He had been thoroughly outfought. The soldiers had also run out of food, and on the return trip his men had to butcher their own horses for food so they wouldn't starve to death.

Again, the Oglalas returned to a life without contact

with whites other than a few traders they allowed to enter their territory with goods. Buffalo abounded— the Oglalas had what they needed.

With news of the unprovoked massacre at Sand Creek and then the killings of Indians on the Plains, whites began to demand better treatment of the Indians. The army had to scale down its plans for all-out war against the "heathens." The kill-on-sight order was no longer followed. Soon another government commission was established to offer the Indians a new peace treaty. They offered the Plains Indians yearly allotments of food, goods, and other gifts. All the treaty asked from the Indians was the right to build and use the Bozeman Trail into Montana and to build forts along the route to protect it.

Most of the Indians heard the terms and didn't sign. They realized that signing meant they would no longer be able to roam their usual hunting grounds. They would have to allow the Bozeman Trail to be opened, and that alone would ruin hunting in a vast section of their lands. They remembered how other trails they had seen and heard about had led to a scarcity of game, then no game at all. They also remembered how all the woods had been cut down—which eventually forced the Indians to leave these areas.

The commissioners said that wouldn't happen here. Some of the minor chiefs (those with small bands) signed with the government and collected their gifts. No Sioux signed.

Almost a year passed and the treaty makers were still waiting for the major chiefs to sign the treaty. Finally in June 1866, several of the leading Sioux chiefs, including Red Cloud, Old-Man-Afraid-of-His-Horses, and Crazy Horse's uncle Spotted Tail, along with some of the other northern Plains tribes' major chiefs, decided that the offer was worth considering. If it meant that the army would stop hunting them down and would give them goods such as guns and ammunition for hunting, it might be worthwhile. They made the trip to Fort Laramie to investigate the treaty for themselves. Crazy Horse argued against their going, pointing out how well they had done in the past year without help from anyone. But Red Cloud was willing to listen to what the white men had to say.

The white commissioners were pleased to finally see the Sioux chiefs and explained in detail how the treaty would work. According to the commissioners, the Indians would receive a great deal for giving up so little. The commissioners offered the Indians guns and ammunition—as the Indians had hoped, because they were always in need of them. The commissioners were also adamant that the treaty would neither let any whites disturb Sioux hunting grounds nor disrupt their nomadic way of life. All the whites wanted was the trail to the Montana Territory.

While they negotiated, Colonel Henry B. Carrington marched into Fort Laramie with the Eighteenth Infantry Regiment of seven hundred men. He claimed his orders were to build forts on the Bozeman Trail regardless of the outcome of the treaty with the Indians. The Indians realized that the government was being two-faced—on the one hand offering peace, on the other hand continuing construction on the trail regardless of the Indians' decision.

Feeling betrayed and angry, Red Cloud echoed in a speech what all the Sioux were feeling. He told the commissioners that the white men had crowded the Indians back year by year until they were forced to live in a small area north of the Platte. Because of the treaty, the army would take away the Indians' hunting grounds, which would mean women and children would starve. Red Cloud said he would rather die by fighting. As he left the council, he said that as long as he lived he would fight the white men for his people's last hunting ground.

All of the Sioux chiefs followed Red Cloud except Spotted Tail, who, a few years earlier, had been captured as a renegade Indian and sent to Fort Leavenworth prison for a year. In prison, he had learned much about the whites, including their massive numbers and their mighty military power. He decided that if the Indians wanted to survive, they must learn to live in peace with the whites.

That summer, Carrington's troops built three forts along the 800-mile-long Bozeman Trail. The first was the rebuilding of Fort Reno near the north fork of the Powder River, 247 miles from Fort Laramie. The second was Carrington's headquarters on Clear Creek, which he named Fort Phil Kearny, 120 miles northwest of Fort Reno. The last one was Fort C. F. Smith, another 130 miles northwest on the Bighorn River.

As Red Cloud and other Sioux watched the whites build the forts, Red Cloud decided the only way to beat the whites was to unite the Plains Indians against this common enemy. He rode from village to village—even to Sioux enemy villages—across the northern Plains with a war pipe asking the Indians to unite for this battle.

By August 1866, Carrington announced to the United States by telegraph and army dispatches that the Bozeman Trail was ready and safe—there were three forts and two thousand troops to protect travelers. Eager gold seekers who had been waiting for the word swarmed the Bozeman Trail.

Red Cloud and his men were ready as well. Red Cloud had two thousand warriors prepared to fight for their families, their way of life, and their last good hunting ground. Crazy Horse, as a Shirt-Wearer and a master of battle tactics, was Red Cloud's top warrior. Red Cloud's Indian raiders hit the route from beginning to end. Riding in small groups, the Indians would strike suddenly and relentlessly, destroying wagon trains, hitting military convoys, and then vanishing into the prairie. They even brazenly broke into the fort corrals and ran off horses and beef cattle.

Crazy Horse, accompanied by Hump, Lone Bear,

Little Hawk, and Young-Man-Afraid-of-His-Horses, led a war party from the hills almost every day. With each raid, Crazy Horse's reputation as a brilliant warrior grew. From August to December of 1866, the Indians killed more than 150 soldiers and civilians and captured several hundred horses, cattle, and mules. To the public, the Bozeman Trail had become known as the "Bloody Bozeman Trail," and traffic on it came to a halt.

The Indians then laid siege to the three forts—soon no white man could venture outside the limits of the army complexes without a strong guarding force. Much of the fighting took place around Fort Phil Kearny, the site of the Battle of the Hundred Slain (the Fetterman Massacre), where a group of Indians led by Crazy Horse lured out eighty soldiers who were then ambushed and killed by two thousand Indians.

After this show of strength by the fearless Indians, the government—still wanting desperately to open the Bozeman Trail—decided they needed a new treaty with the Indians. They worked out a new pact for the Sioux, Cheyennes, and Arapahos. The lands west of the Missouri River, the short-grass prairie, would be given to the Sioux as the Great Sioux Reservation. The government would help the Sioux by setting up agencies on the reservation, building schools, providing clothing and food, and teaching them how to farm the land and raise farm animals. The treaty also stated that the Powder River country would be named

A group of Plains Indians met with U.S. government officials to discuss the Fort Laramie Treaty.

as "unceded Indian territory," and no whites would be allowed to enter it or make claim to it. Any Sioux who wished to pursue buffalo and other wild game could stay there for as long as there were buffalo.

When the snow melted in 1868, several Sioux chiefs visited Fort Laramie and put their marks on the treaty. Crazy Horse, Red Cloud, and the other chiefs and Shirt-Wearers held out, saying it was just another treaty the white men would ignore when they wished to.

Soon, however, Red Cloud sent the commissioners a message. He would put his marks on, or sign, the treaty if the army abandoned the forts they had built to protect the Bozeman Trail. But the army representatives said that would never happen, as the forts were essential to the protection of the area. The commissioners sent word to Washington, D.C., that this demand was impossible to meet.

The politicians in Washington, however, were tired of the Indian wars. Some whites were still angry about the ruthless way the army had been treating the Indians. The politicians decided that the demand could be met. They had another incentive for agreeing to Red Cloud's demand—they wanted to keep the Sioux corralled to the north so they wouldn't endanger construction of the first transcontinental railroad to come through the area. By that time, construction of the rails had progressed well into Sioux country. The politicians could not let this war against the Plains Indians threaten or damage the progress of the railroad that would bind the nation together. The army was ordered to abandon the three forts along the Bozeman Trail. Upon hearing this, Crazy Horse and other warriors rode down from the hills and burned all three forts to the ground.

On November 6, 1868, Red Cloud made his mark on the treaty. True to his word, he told the commissioners that he was ready for peace.

Sitting Bull, Swift Bear, Spotted Tail, front row, left to right, *and Red Cloud,* back row, *at a meeting with an unidentified white man. Perhaps to show their willingness to cooperate with the whites, the Indians—other than Sitting Bull—wore white men's clothing to this meeting.*

Chapter **SEVEN**

AT HOME IN THE POWDER RIVER COUNTRY

THE NEW TREATY WITH THE WHITES HELD. **C**RAZY Horse and the Oglalas were at home in the Powder River country—where game was plentiful, and there were no white men's trails, no army forts, and no soldiers. The Oglalas were doing well; they would survive without the luxury trade goods from government posts. The Sioux lived as their grandfathers had, hunting buffalo and moving with the herds for the big hunt before winter—to fill the parfleches with dried jerky and to take the buffalo robes and other animal parts vital to the Indians' culture and well-being. Crazy Horse knew that he would never go to the reservation. For the time being, he had no contact with whites.

In 1869, Crazy Horse's beloved friend and mentor Hump was killed. The two warriors, along with He Dog, had been raiding a Shoshoni village during snowy, slippery weather when Hump was overwhelmed by a swarm of angry Shoshonis. Crazy Horse was devastated by the loss.

Still, he found a way to carry on. He was a top hunter as well as a warrior. He always divided the buffalo he caught with his family and then with the band's widows and orphans. Unmarried, he still lived in his family's tepee. He had only his one war pony, but sometimes he had a second one he was training. True to his vision quest, he never claimed a share of horses captured in raids or took other bounty from a raid. Rumors circulated in the Oglala bands every so often that Crazy Horse was still in love with Black Buffalo Woman, who by then had three children by No Water, and that she secretly loved Crazy Horse.

By 1869, the Oglalas had more buffalo hides than they could use. During the several years of fighting, the Indians had not traded with the whites—but that summer, some Oglalas went to the trading post at Platte Bridge station with bundles of prime buffalo hides. Soldiers at the trading post warned them that there was no trading permitted along the Platte River, saying that the Indians must trade at a reservation or not at all. The Oglalas insisted, and some of the soldiers opened fire on the trading party, wounding one of the Oglala chiefs. The Indians hurried away.

The Shoshoni Indians were enemies of the Sioux. Pictured above is a Shoshoni chief's tepee.

The U.S. Army had enacted a no-trade order several months earlier, but the Oglalas, having had no contact with whites, didn't know about it. The order had been issued to keep all Indians away from the Oregon Trail and the construction of the nation's first transcontinental railroad, the Union Pacific, across Nebraska and the Rocky Mountains. Whites had begun to violate the 1868 Fort Laramie Treaty by steadily advancing into Indian lands. They also chartered hunting trains and shot buffalo at an alarming rate, rapidly decreasing the animal's population.

Sioux complaints about the treaty violations reached

SIOUX CRAFTS

Women and men in traditional Oglala society specialized in different tribal crafts. Women spent much of their time making clothing from buffalo and deer hides, often decorating them with quills and beads. Occasionally, when the women could find the right clay, they made a small number of pots and fired them in open pits. They did not decorate their pottery.

Women also made parfleches. These were sometimes crafted from buffalo hides. The women would pound on the leather to soften it and use dyes to create designs in the parfleches. Women also wove baskets of many styles and sizes from a variety of grasses, reeds, and strips of tree bark.

Oglala men specialized in crafting bows and arrows, pipes for smoking, warbonnets, and shields. Sometimes a man became so good at making arrows that he devoted all his working hours to making arrows for his tribe's warriors.

Washington, D.C., and government representatives persuaded several of the important Indian leaders to visit Washington and voice their complaints to President Ulysses S. Grant. In 1870, Red Cloud, Spotted Tail, and a number of other Sioux chiefs made the trip by train.

The Sioux leaders were treated like royalty. Government representatives gave the chiefs a grand tour of the city in fancy carriages—with the single purpose of showing them the great power of the government and letting them see for themselves the tremendous number of white people. They visited the Senate, and the chiefs were shown through one of the U.S. arsenal buildings. The chiefs were awestruck by all the rifles they saw there. There were more army rifles in the one building than the chiefs had ever seen in their lifetimes. The power of the new howitzer cannon was demonstrated to them: a huge shell thundered out of the long barrel and flew more than two miles. The howitzers were the most dreaded weapons the Indians had ever seen—one cannonball could kill half a band.

The trip left Red Cloud feeling hopeless. He was now sure that the Indians' armed resistance against the U.S. Army was a fight the Indians couldn't win. Furthermore, he and others knew that the buffalo all across the Plains were being slaughtered by the whites at an astounding rate. Soon they would be gone, even in the Powder River country. When the buffalo disappeared, the Sioux would have to change their ways as well. With all this weighing on their minds, the chiefs returned to the Plains.

In 1871, the government established a special agency, a plot of land near government buildings, for Red Cloud and his followers about thirty miles east of Fort Laramie. Chief Red Cloud went to the agency, took off his warrior clothes and decorations, and never fought as a warrior again. Crazy Horse made it known that he was deeply disappointed with Red Cloud, stating that the Oglalas had not forced the closing of the Bozeman Trail only to quit now and go to a reservation. That would make all of their bloody battles meaningless.

The rest of the Oglalas had a choice to make, too. They could stay in the Powder River country and keep their independence—living by the chase—or they could move to the reservation, give up their independence, and be forever subject to the laws and gifts of the commissioners and Indian leaders who abided by these laws. Many followed Red Cloud, but many others stayed in the Powder River country.

Around this time, the rumors about Crazy Horse and Black Buffalo Woman were turning into truth. Members of the Bad Face band said that Crazy Horse paid open attention to Black Buffalo Woman by walking and talking with her when he visited the band. Though it was uncommon, by Sioux custom a woman could divorce her husband. If a woman did this, her husband was expected to behave well and respect his wife's decision.

One day when No Water was off hunting, Black Buffalo Woman left her children with relatives and rode away from the camp with Crazy Horse. No Water, a jealous man, quickly found out. He took a pistol and rode out to track the eloping couple. He caught up with them at a camp on the Powder River and stormed into the tepee where they were visiting a

Whites hunted buffalo for their skins and for sport, often from trains. As a result, the buffalo were nearly wiped out, leaving the Plains Indians without one of their most valuable resources.

friend. No Water fired at Crazy Horse, hitting him just under his left nostril.

No Water fled the scene and rode back to his village, where he confessed that he had killed Crazy Horse. He went at once into a sweat lodge that had been quickly built for him so he could purify himself from the evil act of murder.

But surprisingly, the bullet had only wounded Crazy Horse—it had broken his jaw. He was immediately taken to an uncle's tepee to be cared for. Black Buffalo Woman scrambled out of the tepee and ran to her relatives, seeking protection. Friends of Crazy Horse searched for No Water but couldn't find him. They took their wrath out on No Water's favorite mule, mutilating it.

In the past, such incidents had destroyed the peace of a tribe. The Big Bellies met to consider the problem. They quickly ruled that Crazy Horse had disgraced himself by putting his own interests first—he had broken his vow as a Shirt-Wearer and had ignored the well-being of the tribe. Crazy Horse was asked to return the ceremonial shirt and the accompanying responsibilities and status of a Shirt-Wearer.

Friends of both injured parties worked quietly to resolve the matter so it wouldn't build into a feud. While Crazy Horse couldn't speak clearly through his broken jaw, he used sign language to tell his friends that there must be no more violence concerning this matter. No Water cooled down and sent three of his best ponies to Crazy Horse's father, Worm, as a gesture of peace. Accepting the horses, Worm agreed that the matter was settled and his family was satisfied. After a lengthy healing process, Crazy Horse was left with a long scar on his face.

Months later, Crazy Horse was out hunting when he happened upon No Water, who was also hunting. Crazy Horse mounted his horse and chased No Water all the way to the Yellowstone River. There, No Water plunged his horse into the water and swam it across the rushing Yellowstone. Soon after, he and Black Buffalo Woman and their children moved permanently to the Red Cloud Agency.

Then tragedy struck again. Crazy Horse's brother Little Hawk had been brutally gunned down by miners—shot in the back and killed. Crazy Horse was angrier than he had ever been. He began to go on hunting trips alone, staying away from camp for days.

Sitting Bull, leader of the Hunkpapa Sioux and ally of Crazy Horse

Chapter **EIGHT**

THE BLACK HILLS

AFTER THE TRAGIC EVENTS OF THE EARLY **1870s,**
Crazy Horse, now in his thirties, became even more
withdrawn. His friends, He Dog and Red Feather, decided it was time for Crazy Horse to marry. They
matched Crazy Horse with a Cheyenne woman named
Black Shawl, Red Feather's sister. Though Crazy Horse
warned Black Shawl that a life with him would bring
her little joy, she accepted the match and they were
married. The two were well suited to each other, and
the marriage was a happy one. Soon they had a baby
daughter whom they named They-Are-Afraid-of-Her.
Enamored with his child, Crazy Horse spent hours
playing with and doting on her.

In the summer of 1872, Crazy Horse and his friend
Sitting Bull, the mighty leader of the Hunkpapa

Sioux, joined forces to challenge the army and a railroad survey party that had come into the Powder River country. The survey party was laying out the route of the Northern Pacific Railroad, which would cut through the northern states and territories—land that the Sioux believed belonged to them. The 1868 Fort Laramie Treaty had not set a northern border on the Indians' "unceded" territory. So the Sioux believed the railroad was a violation of their land.

By midsummer, the railroad survey engineers were approaching the Yellowstone River Valley. The Indians attacked the party. In the end, the Battle of Arrow Creek was a standoff with almost no casualties, but it convinced the railroad men not to do any more work that summer. A short time after this battle, the Oglalas rewarded Crazy Horse for his leadership and battle skills. Crazy Horse was declared war chief of the Oglalas.

The next summer the surveyors returned, this time protected by the Seventh Cavalry under the command of Lieutenant Colonel George Armstrong Custer. Custer was an accomplished army leader. Considered by some whites to be a military genius, at the age of twenty-three he became a general in the Civil War fighting for the North. The title had been intended to be only temporary, and at the end of the war his rank dropped to his regular title of captain. But he was determined to get his rank back—by killing Indians. He had already had some bloody standoffs with the Indians, including the massacre of peaceful Cheyenne villages in the late 1860s.

As the workers laid tracks for transcontinental railroads to the West, many Indian tribes began a series of raids to stop construction across their lands.

During the summer of 1873, there were several furious skirmishes between Custer's men and the Oglalas and other Plains Indians. The soldiers held off the Indians' attacks with their repeating rifles, and the surveying work was soon finished.

In the summer of 1874, Crazy Horse's beloved young daughter died of cholera, a disease spread by the whites. Crazy Horse rode to the platform where her body was laid to rest and lay down beside her for three days. He was inconsolable—he felt the loss so deeply that he was never the same. He became even more soft-spoken and reclusive.

Though the Sioux had lost much of their hunting land, the Black Hills, the sacred center of Sioux culture, was still theirs. According to the 1868 Fort Laramie Treaty, this area was granted to the Sioux "for as long as there are buffalo." For hundreds of years, the Sioux had known that there was gold in the Black Hills. When whites spotted gold there, the government immediately sent Colonel Custer and twelve thousand troops back into the north, this time to confirm the claim. Custer's 1874 report to Congress stated that gold was plentiful in the area.

Well-armed miners and prospectors arrived almost at once. Before the Sioux realized it, there were hundreds, then thousands, of white men swarming the sacred Black Hills. Warriors attacked the miners when and where they could, but the miners resisted the attacks. In Deadwood, one of the hastily built mining towns, a Sioux scalp would sell for three hundred dollars. It seemed as if the miners were in the Black Hills to stay, despite the 1868 treaty.

In 1875, government representatives announced to the Indians that they wanted to buy the Black Hills from the Sioux. Red Cloud and Spotted Tail were invited back to Washington, D.C. There, they were persuaded and then threatened—if the Indians didn't agree to sell the Black Hills, there was no way that the army could keep the gold miners and prospectors out of the area. The chiefs said they must return home to discuss the matter.

In August, government commissioners went to Sioux country and arranged a council to discuss the Black

Hills. Some of the Sioux, led by Crazy Horse and Sitting Bull, didn't live on a reservation and would have nothing to do with selling the Black Hills. Some others, led by Red Cloud, who lived on an agency were ready to sell. A third group, led by Young-Man-Afraid-of-His-Horses who also lived on an agency, did not want to sell.

In fall of 1875, the Lone Tree Council began to discuss the issue. Thousands of Indians came to watch. At one point, a group of enraged Sioux warriors rode into the middle of the council circle on horseback and violently circled and whooped around the commissioners to show their opposition—until Young-Man-Afraid-of-His-Horses finally persuaded them to cool off. The council deliberated for several days. The government offered the Indians six million dollars for the Black Hills. The chiefs refused to sell their sacred land for what seemed like pennies. In the end, no agreement was reached.

Secret meetings in Washington between the Bureau of Indian Affairs and Congress decided the issue. The Indians would be forced out of their remaining non-reservation land in the Powder River country (including the Black Hills) and resettled on agencies. In December, runners from the government went out to all the Powder River bands. They were told that they must report to an Indian agency by January 31, 1876, or the U.S. Army would march against them and force them onto reservations.

The massive encampment of Plains Indians along the Little
Bighorn River before the Battle of the Little Bighorn

Chapter **NINE**

THE BATTLE OF THE LITTLE BIGHORN

THE SNOW WAS DEEP IN THE YEAR OF **1876.** THE
Sioux and other Plains Indians did not understand
why they should try to move in midwinter. It was
never done. Many people and ponies would inevitably
die. They decided that they would wait until spring
and then negotiate with the government—this was
their land and no government official could tell them
where to go and what to do.

Early in February 1876, the army sent "Three Stars"
General George C. Crook with ten companies of cavalry and two companies of infantry to march north to
round up the Indians. Crook was described as ruthless
in war but fatherly and humane in peacetime.

The soldiers first came upon a band of Northern

Cheyennes. Their chief, Old Bear, decided it would be better to surrender and go to a reservation than to fight the army. Before the Cheyennes began to move toward the fort to surrender, they were found by army scouts. In temperatures falling below zero, six companies of cavalry launched a surprise attack on the Indian camp. The sudden attack caught most of the warriors still buttoned up inside their tepees for warmth. When they realized what was happening, they quickly scrambled out. Women and children ran up the hills on both sides of the valley. Then the warriors counterattacked with such force that the soldiers gave way—but only after the Indian village had been burned and virtually everything had been destroyed. For three days the survivors walked downstream through the snow and bitter cold to Crazy Horse's camp, where he took them in.

The attack ignited Crazy Horse to continue what Red Cloud had begun—uniting the Plains Indians against the whites. He soon took his Oglalas far to the north where he teamed up with Sitting Bull. Other bands from all over the Powder River area soon came to join them. It was steadily becoming one great Sioux gathering to discuss war against the whites.

Sitting Bull sent runners to agencies and reservations, encouraging Indians living there to leave and come north and join them in the great fight to throw the white man out of Indian country. Having spent months or years on reservations and agencies, many

Indians were not pleased with this life, and thousands soon left and headed north. Crazy Horse sent the same message to other Plains tribes. In May 1876, the encampment grew to more than twelve thousand Indians. Every day more fighters and their families from the agencies came north and joined the massive gathering of the tribes. Feeling strong and confident in their unity, the tribes feasted, danced, and sang together. Soon there were so many Indians and ponies that they had to move every few days to find new grazing land for the animals.

That June, the encampment celebrated the most spectacular Sun Dance in Plains history. Warriors pierced their bodies. Bleeding and elated, they danced the Sun Dance. Sitting Bull offered his body to *Wakan Tanka*. After Sitting Bull had fifty pieces of flesh cut from his body, he danced around the sacred pole for eighteen hours before he fainted. When he awoke, he told the encampment about the vision he had—soldiers were going to attack the Indians' camp, and that the soldiers would be killed.

The army knew of the gathering, but the generals didn't know that there were so many thousands of Indians or what their exact location was. The U.S. government was determined to force all the Indians onto reservations once and for all. So the army began a march toward the Powder River country. As the Indians gathered, the army assembled the largest force ever used against the Indians. A three-pronged unit led by General Crook, General John Gibbon, and Lieutenant Colonel Custer (whom Crazy Horse had fought in the Yellowstone River Valley) continued toward the encampment.

Just a few days after the grand Sun Dance, on June 16, Cheyenne scouts reported that Crook and twelve hundred soldiers, led by Crow (longtime Sioux and Cheyenne enemies) scouts, were fast approaching their camp at Ash Creek. Crazy Horse and other Sioux and Cheyenne leaders came together in an emergency meeting. They decided they were ready to fight.

Crazy Horse, taking on his role as war chief, directed half of the warriors to stay back and protect the camp, while the rest—sixteen hundred Cheyenne and Sioux warriors—began a night march so they could surprise the army troops at dawn. As the sun rose over the Rosebud Creek Valley, the warriors found Crook and his soldiers—and charged. The alert Crow scouts fought off this attack. But the Sioux and Cheyennes attacked the soldiers again and again. Crazy Horse instructed his warriors to abandon their usual hit-and-run tactics, which would have provided them with individual honor and glory. Instead, they attacked as a massive, strong, united force. The battle continued well into the afternoon.

The Sioux and Cheyenne Indians fought with great ferocity and skill, pulling back only after they began to run out of ammunition. Crook and his forces, who were also weary and low on ammunition, retreated.

Both of the war parties considered the day a victory.

Toward the end of June 1876, the tribal circles of te-pees edged along the Little Bighorn River, where the Sioux and Northern Cheyennes had moved their camp. Tepees extended back as far as a mile from the water, for three miles. Each tribe had its assigned place in the camp. The Cheyennes were at the north-ern end, and other tribes extended south, led by the Brules and Oglalas, with the Hunkpapas at the south-ern end. Never in the memory of the oldest warriors had there ever been this many Indians—thousands and thousands—at one place, ready to make war on a single enemy.

On June 25, 1876, while women, children, and hunters were going about their daily business, the war chiefs were receiving continual updates from scouts about the whereabouts of Custer and Gibbon, both on the track of the Indian camp. Custer was moving west toward the Little Bighorn River.

Custer had more than six hundred cavalry soldiers armed with carbines and pistols, and thirty-five Crow and Shoshoni scouts. Unbeknownst to Crazy Horse, two miles from the village Custer split his command into three parts. He sent the first part—led by Major Marcus A. Reno, one of Custer's trusted officers—directly to the river. Reno was to cross it, come up the valley, and attack the village from the south, the Hunkpapa's end. A second section, led by Captain Frederick Benteen, would scout along the foot of the

Wolf Mountains to cut off any escaping Indians, then ride up as a reinforcement for Reno. Custer himself would take his men along the bluff on the east side of the river, cross it farther downstream, and attack the north end of the camp.

The Battle of the Little Bighorn began when Reno crossed the river where instructed, then charged up the open valley toward the south end of the camp where the Hunkpapas were settled. The cavalry soldiers had a two-mile ride once they broke into the open of the valley.

The Indian lookouts shrilled out the warning and it passed from one camp to the next as soon as they saw the soldiers coming. They called, "The chargers are coming, they are charging!" Everyone in the camp, even Crazy Horse, was caught off guard. As a first priority, women and children were hurried out of the camp, away from the bullets. Warriors rushed around getting just enough war paint on to protect themselves, then they grabbed their rifles, lances, war clubs, or bows and arrows.

As they charged forward, the cavalry fired their carbines, shooting into the tepees from the galloping horses. Just outside the village, the cavalry stopped, dismounted, and formed a line of men side by side, ready to shoot.

With the women and children safely away from the fighting, mounted warriors rushed to meet the enemy. They rode up and down in front of the line of soldiers, forcing them to quickly retreat to a grove of cotton-wood trees along the river. About then, Crazy Horse, wearing his breechcloth, his lightning paint on one cheek, appeared on his yellow war pony shouting for the warriors to conserve bullets, as they had far less ammunition than the whites. He rallied more warriors from the camp and led scores of them into the fight, pressing the cavalrymen deeper into the woods. The soldiers were hiding behind rocks and trees, but the Indians kept coming. Just before they were overrun,

In his relentless pursuit of Crazy Horse and other "hostile" Indians, Lieutenant Colonel George A. Custer (center) *often used members of the Crow and Shoshoni tribes as scouts.*

Major Reno ordered the troops to withdraw to the steep bluffs on the other side of the river.

The soldiers mounted their horses and rode in disarray and in full retreat across the flat valley to the river. The Sioux pounded after them on their light, fast ponies, catching many of them and knocking them off their mounts with tomahawks and rifles. Moments later, Captain Benteen's soldiers arrived to reinforce Reno. The Indians however, far outnumbered the soldiers. Before the Indians could launch their killing attack on Reno and Benteen, they spotted Custer's blue-coated cavalry on the bluff high over the village, riding north.

Remarkably, Crazy Horse managed to persuade his warriors to leave a guaranteed victory—they had an even greater battle ahead of them for which to prepare. At once, the warriors left the soldiers they had been fighting and rode north through the village to meet this new threat.

From the ridge, Custer could see and hear the first part of Reno's attack on the south end of the village. Custer hurried to a long ravine about halfway along the village. It led downward from the ridge and opened into a broad valley. At the bottom of this, Custer would cross the Little Bighorn River and attack the camp. He didn't realize this path would bring him to about the middle of the three-mile-long encampment. Once he rode down the valley, he sent two companies charging toward the river. They ran into heavy rifle fire from Indians hiding in brush across the creek. The soldiers faded back in the face of the heavy fire.

Dozens more Indians came to support those in the brush—then hundreds came, many from the battle with Reno. A Hunkpapa chief named Gall led a large group of warriors who charged across the river to attack. The soldiers were badly outnumbered and fell back, fighting as they went, and angled up to the high ridge known as Battle Ridge, with Gall's men following.

Back in the village, Crazy Horse raced through the circles of tents, screaming at those warriors not yet in the fight. He led these hundreds of fighters toward the north end of the village. The group galloped through the camp, crossed the river, and charged up a ravine to

In the Battle of the Little Bighorn, Chief Gall, a leader of the Hunkpapa Sioux, and his warriors forced Major Reno's troops to retreat.

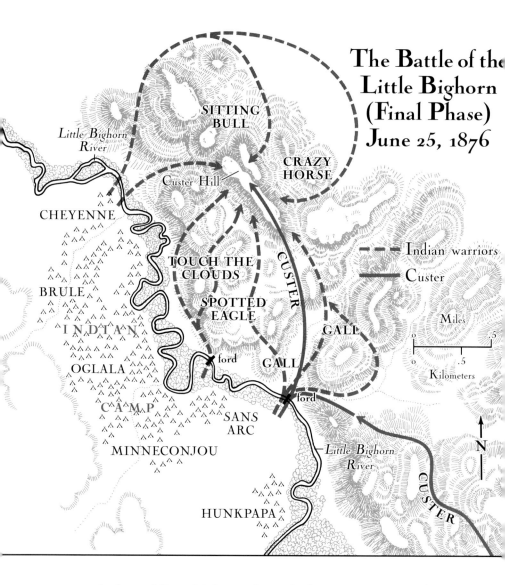

The Battle of the
Little Bighorn
(Final Phase)
June 25, 1876

Little Bighorn
River

SITTING
BULL

CRAZY
HORSE

Custer Hill

CHEYENNE

TOUCH THE
CLOUDS

CUSTER

- - - Indian warriors
——— Custer

BRULE

SPOTTED
EAGLE

INDIAN

GALL

Miles

0   .5

OGLALA

ford

GALL

0   .5

Kilometers

CAMP

SANS
ARC

MINNECONJOU

Little Bighorn
River

ford

N

HUNKPAPA

CUSTER

attack the soldiers high on the ridgeline. Crazy Horse's
strategy was for his warriors to attack the soldiers' rear
instead of the frontal attack they probably expected.

On the ridge, the warriors with Gall worked forward,
attacking the cavalry wherever they found them. At

last, some of the soldiers dismounted and formed a skirmish line to stop the Indians' advance.

Soon, Custer's men were spread out along the ridge in a thin line. The warriors hid behind rocks, high grass, and sage, firing bullets and arrows at the unprotected cavalrymen. In some places the soldiers were clustered together for better protection, but even these men began to die by twos and threes, then by the dozen.

Before Custer could gather his men to retreat along the ridge to a small rise at the far end, Crazy Horse and his warriors attacked from the rear. The Indians surged toward the outnumbered and weary soldiers. The soldiers fought for their lives. They had never seen so many Indians. The cavalrymen fired from behind dead horses, from saddles piled two or three high, and from the protection of a few rocks. Dust from the ponies' hooves and gun smoke soon clouded the hilltop. A few soldiers tried to break out and run down the hill. They were shot. Other soldiers were clubbed to death or fell in hand-to-hand combat with the Indians.

It is not known whether Crazy Horse and Custer, the two war leader enemies, recognized one another on the field. Custer (known by the Indians as Long Hair) had cut his hair, and Crazy Horse blended in with the other painted warriors in the dust and frenzy of the battle. Once the warriors charged across the last defensive line of Custer's soldiers, the battle was over.

Sioux artist Kicking Bear, a survivor of the Battle of the Little Bighorn, painted his recollection of that fight. The outlined figures at top left represent spirits escaping from the bodies of the dead and dying soldiers.

Every soldier, including the ruthless Custer, lay dead in the dust of the ridge and hill. In two hours, the Indians had achieved their greatest victory against the whites in decades of fighting.

But the fight was not yet over. Below the ridge three miles to the south, Reno and Benteen's troops had dug holes to hide in and protect themselves. Warriors, fresh from the victory on the hill against Custer, galloped on their horses to finish off these men. The Indians still had ammunition and carbines left, and they kept up a steady rain of fire on the soldiers. But Reno and Benteen's soldiers held off the Indian attack until nightfall, giving the soldiers eight hours of darkness to dig deeper and better holes to improve their defenses. The soldiers had plenty of ammunition, and their cliff-top position would be hard to overrun.

During the morning, the Indians continued their attack. Just after noon, Indian scouts reported seeing a long column of blue-coated soldiers—Gibbon's cavalry—riding up the valley to reinforce the trapped soldiers.

Crazy Horse and Sitting Bull held a council. Deciding that there had been enough killing, they left Reno and Benteen's troops, broke camp, and headed for new hunting grounds.

When General Gibbon and his troops rode into the deserted camping area, the Indians were gone. Only dead soldiers' bodies remained.

The Battle of the Little Bighorn was the greatest disaster suffered by the United States Army in all of its Indian wars. There would be years of accusations, finger pointing, and attempts to assign the blame. Only the Indians knew for certain what happened at what came to be known by the whites as Custer's Last Stand.

Shown above is a telegram from the United States Army in Washington, D.C., to a general in Chicago, requesting clarification of reports on Custer's fate.

Chapter **TEN**

SACRIFICE

THE GREATEST GATHERING OF PLAINS INDIAN WARRIORS in history had come to a close. Though the people at the massive encampment tried to stay together, bands began breaking off to go to different camping grounds or even back to the agencies and reservations.

Crazy Horse thought that after the Indians' great victory, the white men would think twice before challenging the Indians. But just the opposite was true. Public opinion now favored the U.S. Army. The public demanded that the guilty Indians pay a price for the slaying of Custer and his troops. The army soon established new forts on the Yellowstone River and sent armies of skilled and determined soldiers to continue the attacks meant to capture the Indians who still refused to enter the reservations. Afraid for their lives, even more Indians returned to their agencies and reservations.

Ever fearless, Crazy Horse returned to the Black Hills to raid miners and settlers. In late 1876, while Crazy Horse was fighting to defend the Black Hills, Red Cloud, Spotted Tail, and other chiefs who had stayed in agencies during the Custer fight, were pressured by the whites into signing away the sacred Black Hills. Upon hearing the news that the chiefs had given up this land, Crazy Horse was horrified, feeling betrayed by the chiefs.

That winter, several important army leaders sought to capture Crazy Horse and Sitting Bull, whom the whites saw as fugitives. Crook, the general who destroyed Old Bear's peaceful Northern Cheyenne village, went after Crazy Horse. Crook promised a gun and a horse to any warrior on the Red Cloud Agency who would act as a scout to help hunt down Crazy Horse. Sixty warriors agreed to go—among them was No Water.

During his mission, Crook happened upon a Cheyenne village. He and his army attacked and destroyed it. Then Crook burned the village and sent the survivors running into the hills. It took the survivors two agonizing weeks in freezing weather, clamoring through the deep snow, before they found Crazy Horse. Crazy Horse's Oglalas took them in and shared with them what food they had. But the Oglalas had already been reduced to eating their ponies. Food was scarce because there had been little time for the traditional buffalo hunt in the fall. Also, the buffalo were vanishing as the white men continued to shoot them.

Some Oglalas decided to surrender. The rest of Crazy Horse's band moved higher on the Tongue River. Feeling a growing powerlessness against the weapons and masses of whites, Crazy Horse began to consider putting his pride aside and doing what he had to do to ensure his people's survival—surrendering. It was becoming impossible for his people to fight the army all the time and still try to live by the old ways of hunting buffalo or other wild animals.

Near the end of December 1876, Crazy Horse took his band toward the army camp of Colonel Nelson A. Miles, who had been pursuing Sitting Bull's Hunkpapas. Crazy Horse stopped near the camp and sent a delegation under a flag of truce to talk with the army about his possible surrender. The colonel's Crow scouts recognized the hated Oglala delegation and charged them, killing five. The Oglalas fled. The colonel, eager to have Crazy Horse surrender to *him*, was furious with the Crows and took away their horses. He set out to capture Crazy Horse himself.

For the rest of the winter, Crazy Horse's Oglalas dodged the army and tried to find enough food to stay alive. More and more non-reservation bands were surrendering to the whites.

The army began sending out delegates to urge the holdouts to come in for warm shelter and plenty of food. Finally, Crazy Horse agreed to surrender when the weather permitted. His people, who numbered more than one thousand including three hundred warriors, were tired and hungry.

On April 27, Red Cloud, as ardent as the whites for Crazy Horse's surrender, set out to find him, bringing along one hundred wagonloads of food and gifts for the starving Oglalas. On May 6, 1877, Red Cloud brought Crazy Horse and his people into the Red Cloud Agency, where Crazy Horse formally surrendered. When the warriors dismounted, soldiers from nearby Camp Robinson stepped up and took the warriors' horses and guns.

About the same time, the last Sioux disappeared from the Powder River country. Sitting Bull and his Hunkpapas had crossed the border into Canada. A few days after this, Colonel Miles caught up with a small camp of the Minneconjou tribe of Sioux near the Tongue River and captured them. The U.S. government's wars with the Sioux had ended.

Crazy Horse was miserable on the Red Cloud Agency. He had given up his weapons and his horse, given up his ability to roam the countryside and hunt, given up the freedom he had cherished for thirty-six years.

Crazy Horse lived in a lodge near Camp Robinson and had been promised a future agency of his own.

Young warriors at the camp idolized Crazy Horse, as he had never been defeated by the U.S. Army and because he was gracious and generous. Most of the agency Indians knew that Crazy Horse never kept anything for himself. Soon, fascinated army officers began to stop by to meet the man who defeated Custer.

All of this attention began to wear on Red Cloud. He became envious of Crazy Horse, considering him a rival as the chief of all the Oglalas. The Oglalas had no top chief, but Red Cloud had given himself the title and he worried that Crazy Horse would want it. Red Cloud began spreading rumors that Crazy Horse planned to kill General Crook, take his people and leave the agency.

Upon hearing this, the soldiers and officers at the small army detachment at Camp Robinson grew angry and mistrustful. Soon an order went out to arrest Crazy Horse. He heard about it, borrowed horses, and rode away with Black Shawl to Spotted Tail's agency fifty miles away.

One thousand men were sent to capture him and bring him back. Spotted Tail persuaded him to return. Spotted Tail and Touch-the-Clouds rode on each side of him. They promised that he would receive a fair hearing back at the Red Cloud Agency. When they reached Camp Robinson, thousands of Indians were milling around, waiting to see what would be done with Crazy Horse.

Lieutenant William Clark, the military commander

of the Red Cloud Agency, tried to take Crazy Horse to see Camp Robinson's commander so Crazy Horse could receive a fair hearing as he had been promised. But orders had been given to arrest him and put him in the guardhouse until he could be sent to Omaha, Nebraska, and then on to some post where he could no longer cause trouble.

Several Indians, including Crazy Horse's old friend He Dog, eager to show the whites that they could be useful to them, came to escort Crazy Horse inside the guardhouse. Crazy Horse thought they were going to see the colonel.

Just what happened after that is still not clear. Some say that as Crazy Horse saw that he was being led toward the room with the bars and ball and chain, he realized that he was about to be locked into a tiny cell. He pulled loose from his guards, drew a knife from under his blanket, and charged toward the door and freedom, slashing at anyone who came in his way. One of the guards, probably Little Big Man, caught Crazy Horse from behind in a bear hug, pinning his arms against his sides. But Crazy Horse struggled free and surged through the door and out of the guardhouse.

Officers began shouting for the soldiers to kill Crazy Horse. Little Big Man, catching up to Crazy Horse, held him as a white officer stabbed him with a bayonet. Crazy Horse stiffened, then fell to the ground, still alive.

A painting of Oglala Sioux men and women taking Crazy Horse's body, wrapped in cloth, to a gravesite near Camp Sheridan, Nebraska. Later, members of the Oglalas moved the body to an unknown site.

He Dog and Touch-the-Clouds rushed up to Crazy Horse. Blood gushed from the wound in his back the moment the soldier's bayonet was withdrawn. Touch-the-Clouds, the seven-foot-tall chief, gently carried Crazy Horse into the army assistant's office where they lay him on a red blanket. Crazy Horse asked to be laid on the ground, to be closer to the earth. The army surgeon gave him morphine to ease his pain as Crazy Horse slipped in and out of consciousness. Worm was summoned, and he knelt at his son's side.

About an hour later, Touch-the-Clouds walked out of the office and looked at the crowd in the moonlight. He told them that Chief Crazy Horse had flown from this life to meet *Wakan Tanka*—he was dead.

Jealousy, rumors, envy, and lies by his own people had brought down one of the Oglala Sioux's greatest warriors and war leaders. His own people had done to him what the whole United States Army in fifteen years of fighting couldn't do.

THE LIFE OF CRAZY HORSE

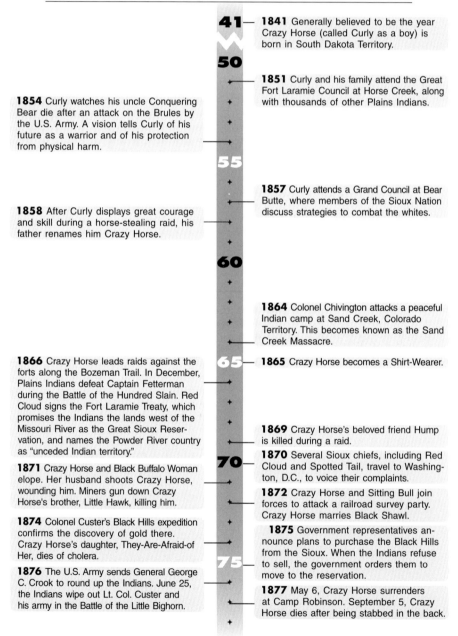

41 — **1841** Generally believed to be the year Crazy Horse (called Curly as a boy) is born in South Dakota Territory.

50

1851 Curly and his family attend the Great Fort Laramie Council at Horse Creek, along with thousands of other Plains Indians.

1854 Curly watches his uncle Conquering Bear die after an attack on the Brules by the U.S. Army. A vision tells Curly of his future as a warrior and of his protection from physical harm.

55

1857 Curly attends a Grand Council at Bear Butte, where members of the Sioux Nation discuss strategies to combat the whites.

1858 After Curly displays great courage and skill during a horse-stealing raid, his father renames him Crazy Horse.

60

1864 Colonel Chivington attacks a peaceful Indian camp at Sand Creek, Colorado Territory. This becomes known as the Sand Creek Massacre.

1866 Crazy Horse leads raids against the forts along the Bozeman Trail. In December, Plains Indians defeat Captain Fetterman during the Battle of the Hundred Slain. Red Cloud signs the Fort Laramie Treaty, which promises the Indians the lands west of the Missouri River as the Great Sioux Reservation, and names the Powder River country as "unceded Indian territory."

65 — **1865** Crazy Horse becomes a Shirt-Wearer.

1869 Crazy Horse's beloved friend Hump is killed during a raid.

1870 Several Sioux chiefs, including Red Cloud and Spotted Tail, travel to Washington, D.C., to voice their complaints.

1871 Crazy Horse and Black Buffalo Woman elope. Her husband shoots Crazy Horse, wounding him. Miners gun down Crazy Horse's brother, Little Hawk, killing him.

70

1872 Crazy Horse and Sitting Bull join forces to attack a railroad survey party. Crazy Horse marries Black Shawl.

1874 Colonel Custer's Black Hills expedition confirms the discovery of gold there. Crazy Horse's daughter, They-Are-Afraid-of Her, dies of cholera.

1875 Government representatives announce plans to purchase the Black Hills from the Sioux. When the Indians refuse to sell, the government orders them to move to the reservation.

1876 The U.S. Army sends General George C. Crook to round up the Indians. June 25, the Indians wipe out Lt. Col. Custer and his army in the Battle of the Little Bighorn.

75

1877 May 6, Crazy Horse surrenders at Camp Robinson. September 5, Crazy Horse dies after being stabbed in the back.

SELECTED BIBLIOGRAPHY

Ambrose, Stephen E. *Crazy Horse and Custer: The Parallel Lives of Two American Warriors.* New York: Anchor Books, 1996.

Blevins, Winfred. *Stone Song: A Novel of the Life of Crazy Horse.* New York: Tom Doherty Associates, 1996.

Brady, Cyrus Townsend. *Indian Fights and Fighters.* Lincoln: University of Nebraska Press, 1971.

Brown, Dee. *Bury My Heart at Wounded Knee.* New York: Holt, Reinhart & Winston, 1971.

Brown, Vinson. *Crazy Horse, Hoka Hey! It Is a Good Time to Die.* Happy Camp, CA: Naturegraph Publishing Inc., 1987.

Buecker, Thomas, ed., and R. Eli Paul. *The Crazy Horse Surrender Ledger.* Lincoln: Nebraska State Historical Society, 1994.

Capps, Benjamin. *The Indians.* Old West Series. New York: Time Life Books, 1973.

Clark, Robert A., ed. *The Killing of Chief Crazy Horse: Three Eyewitness Views.* Lincoln: University of Nebraska Press, 1976.

Connell, Evan S. *Son of the Morning Star: Custer and the Little Bighorn.* San Francisco: North Point Press, 1984.

Dugan, Bill. *Crazy Horse.* New York: Harper Collins, 1992.

Freedman, Russell. *The Life and Death of Crazy Horse.* New York: Holiday House, 1996.

Garst, Shannon. *Crazy Horse.* Boston: Houghton Mifflin, 1950.

Goldman, Martin S. *Crazy Horse, War Chief of the Oglala Sioux.* Danbury, CT: Franklin Watts, 1996.

Guttmacher, Peter. *Crazy Horse: Sioux War Chief.* North American Indians of Achievement Series. New York: Chelsea House, 1994.

Hinman, Eleanor. *Oglala Sources on the Life of Crazy Horse.* Lincoln: Nebraska State Historical Society, 1976.

Kadlecek Edward & Mabell. *To Kill an Eagle: Indian Views on the Last Days of Crazy Horse.* Boulder, CO: Johnson Books, 1991.

Matthiessen, Peter. *In the Spirit of Crazy Horse.* New York: Viking Penguin, 1992.

McMurtry, Larry. *Crazy Horse.* New York: Viking Penguin, 1999.

Meadowcroft, Enid LaMonte. *Crazy Horse.* Champaign, IL: Garrard Publications Company, 1965.

Neihardt, John G. *Black Elk Speaks.* Lincoln: University of Nebraska Press, 1961.

Nightengale, Robert. *Little Big Horn.* Minneapolis: Far West Publishing Corporation, 1996.

Sandoz, Mari. *Crazy Horse, The Strange Man of the Oglala.* Lincoln: University of Nebraska Press, 1992.

St. George, Judith. *Crazy Horse.* New York: Putnam, 1994.

Stroutenburgh, John Jr. *Dictionary of the American Indian.* New York: Philosophical Library, 1960.

Utley, Robert M. *Frontier Regulars, The United States Army and the Indian, 1866-1891.* New York: Macmillan, 1973.

INDEX

AUTHOR ACKNOWLEDGMENTS

Anyone who writes about Crazy Horse is indebted to Mari Sandoz, the author of the definitive biography of Crazy Horse: *Crazy Horse, The Strange Man of the Oglala*. Sandoz established a remarkable base of information about Crazy Horse from the Indian viewpoint. Every author of books or articles on Crazy Horse owes Mari Sandoz an unrepayable debt of gratitude.

OTHER TITLES FROM LERNER AND A&E®:

Arthur Ashe
Bill Gates
Bruce Lee
Christopher Reeve
George Lucas
Gloria Estefan
Jacques Cousteau
Jesse Owens
Jesse Ventura
John Glenn
Legends of Dracula
Louisa May Alcott

Madeleine Albright
Maya Angelou
Mother Teresa
Nelson Mandela
Princess Diana
Queen Cleopatra
Rosie O'Donnell
Saint Joan of Arc
Wilma Rudolph
Women in Space
Women of the Wild West

ABOUT THE AUTHOR

Chet Cunningham is the author of more than two hundred novels and nonfiction books. He is married with two grown children. He and his wife, Rose Marie, live in San Diego, California, where he continues to write. In 1994, he founded the nonprofit organization San Diego Book Awards Association to recognize local writers of books. From this stems the successful Read-4-Fun program aimed at fifth graders to encourage them to read more.

PHOTO ACKNOWLEDGMENTS

The images in this book are used with the permission of: Archive Photos, pp. 2, 6, 14, 17 (left), 34, 46, 49, 71; Nebraska State Historical Society/RG2955-27, p. 10; Smithsonian Institution, National Anthropological Archives, pp. 17 (right) (3700), 54 (56,630); Wyoming Div. of Cultural Resources, p. 18; The Walters Art Gallery, Baltimore, p. 22; Center for Southwest Research, University of New Mexico, p. 26; Denver Public Library, Western History Collection, pp. 30, 53, 105; National Archives, pp. 33 (NWDNS-101-IN-3143A), 41 (NWDNS-111-SC-87740), 66 (111-SC-95986), 98 (NWCTB-94-CORR-PI17E12-3770); South Dakota Historical Society—State Archives, pp. 38, 58; Library of Congress, pp. 51 (LC-B8171-0290), 71 (LC-34815 262-8886), 78 (LC-USZ62-3215); Brown Brothers, pp. 68, 93; Union Pacific Railroad, p. 81; Colorado State Historical Society, p. 84; Northern Pacific Railway Company, p. 91; Southwest Museum, Los Angeles. Photo # CT.1/1026.G.1, p. 96. Front cover: Colorado State Historical Society, (Publisher enhanced with sepia tone). Back cover: Museum of the South Dakota State Historical Society, Pierre, SD.